Recycling Adds Up

By Pam Zollman

WE
RECYCLE

CELEBRATION PRESS

Pearson Learning Group

Contents

What Is Garbage?

Garbage is anything that people throw away. Each day a person throws away about $4\frac{1}{2}$ pounds of garbage. That's the weight of more than three basketballs! That's a lot of garbage.

In fact, the amount of garbage people throw away is huge. Each year in the United States, there is enough garbage to fill garbage trucks from Earth halfway to the Moon! Garbage has become a big problem.

Each day, lots of garbage is thrown away.

3

What Do We Throw Away?

Can you guess what material is found most often in garbage? It's paper! In fact, for every 100 pounds of garbage, more than 40 pounds of it is paper. Wrapping paper, cereal boxes, newspapers, and many other paper items become garbage. Look at the chart on the next page to see other items that make up garbage.

Paper Facts

- Most people in the United States use between 500 and 600 pounds of paper per year.
- Every year in the United States 900 million trees are cut down to make paper.
- Every day, American businesses use enough paper to circle Earth about 20 times.

More paper is found in garbage than any other material.

What's in Garbage

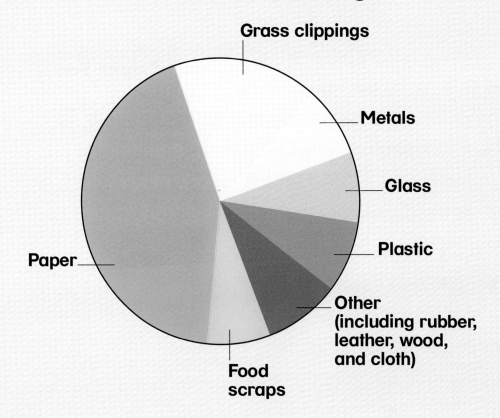

- A little more than $\frac{4}{10}$ of garbage is paper.
- Less than $\frac{2}{10}$ is grass clippings.
- Less than $\frac{1}{10}$ is food scraps.

- Less than $\frac{1}{10}$ is metals.
- Less than $\frac{1}{10}$ is glass.
- Less than $\frac{1}{10}$ is plastic.
- A little more than $\frac{1}{10}$ is rubber, leather, wood, and cloth.

Landfills

Where does garbage go? Most garbage is brought to **landfills**. Landfills take up a lot of space. They can be as large as hundreds of football fields. They can also be very tall. In fact, one landfill in Ohio is about 300 feet tall. That's almost as tall as the Statue of Liberty in New York City!

garbage deposited in a landfill

A Diagram of a Modern Landfill

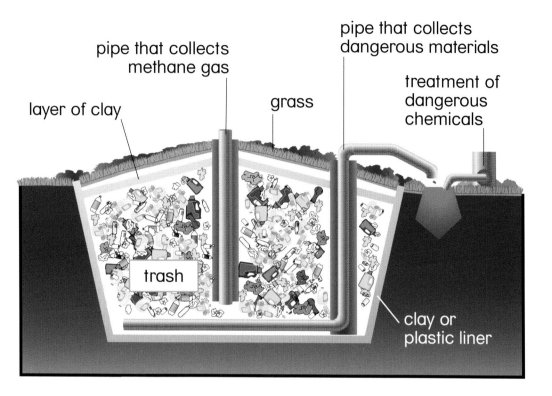

pipe that collects methane gas

pipe that collects dangerous materials

treatment of dangerous chemicals

layer of clay

grass

trash

clay or plastic liner

Burying garbage in landfills might cause problems. Dangerous chemicals from rotting garbage might seep through into the soil. Land and water sources can become polluted. Also, rotting garbage can cause gases to build up. A dangerous gas called methane makes up about half of the gases in landfills. Methane can cause explosions!

Garbage Can Be Recycled

An important solution to handling garbage is **recycling**. Recycling means making something already used into the same thing or something different.

About $\frac{3}{10}$ of garbage in the United States is recycled. Examples of things that can be recycled include glass, **aluminum** cans, and paper. A glass jelly jar can be crushed to make a glass juice bottle. Your notebook paper can be recycled to make greeting cards.

The triangular recycling symbol is printed on some objects that can be recycled.

Recycling Is Important

Recycling is important for many reasons. One reason is that it reduces the amount of garbage in landfills. Paper, metal, glass, wood, and plastic make up about $\frac{7}{10}$ of garbage. Recycling these items saves a lot of space in landfills.

Disposable Diapers

A baby usually wears diapers for 2 to 3 years and can use more than 8,000 diapers. Disposable diapers can last hundreds of years in a landfill.

Things that can be recycled should be sorted and put out for collection.

Another reason recycling is important is because it can prevent trees from being cut down. Did you know that it takes a 15-year-old tree to make 700 paper grocery bags? Instead of cutting down trees, people could use grocery bags made from recycled paper. Thousands of trees could be saved.

Many trees could be saved if more paper was recycled.

Save a Tree

Recycling the amount of paper in a 3-foot-high stack of newspapers can save a tree.

Saving **energy** is another reason why recycling is important. Recycling aluminum is a good example of saving energy. Aluminum is found in a certain type of rock. To get the aluminum, the rock needs to be heated to a very high temperature. It takes a lot of energy to remove aluminum from the rock.

However, recycling an aluminum can to make new aluminum products takes less than $\frac{1}{10}$ the energy of heating rocks. That's a lot of energy that can be saved! Recycling glass and paper can also save energy.

Facts About Aluminium

- Aluminum can be recycled over and over again.

- Recycling one aluminum can instead of making a new one saves enough energy to run a TV for about 3 hours.

- After 500 years, an aluminum can that is deposited in a landfill will remain an aluminum can.

Other Ways to Recycle

There are other ways that garbage is recycled. For example, **composting** recycles grass clippings and food scraps. These items are mixed together in compost piles. After a while, the materials turn into rich soil. The soil can be added to gardens to help plants grow.

In a compost pile, worms and bacteria help turn grass clippings and food scraps into rich soil.

Glass, paper, and aluminum items aren't the only things that can be recycled. Items made of plastic can be recycled to make furniture, building materials, and outdoor play-sets. Some batteries can be recycled, too. Recharging certain types of old batteries allows them to be used again. Even used motor oil can be recycled and burned to produce heat or electricity.

This buffalo sculpture is made from recycled items.

Recycling is a great way to handle garbage. When people recycle, less garbage is put in landfills. Many materials are saved, and less energy can be used. In the future, garbage could be less of a problem if more garbage is recycled.

Recycling can be hard work, but it's worth it!

Glossary

aluminum   a type of metal that can be used over and over again to make new products

composting   mixing grass clippings and food scraps to produce a rich soil

energy   power needed to make something

garbage   anything that people throw away

landfills   large areas where garbage is deposited

recycling   making something already used into the same thing or something different

Index